*Happy 1st Birthday Charles Edward
Edmund, Emmelyn, Ann & Paul.*

ANNIE'S
abc

ANNIE OWEN

ORCHARD BOOKS
London & New York

For Philippa,
and
for Tom and Huw

Text and illustrations copyright © Annie Owen 1987
First published in Great Britain 1987 by
ORCHARD BOOKS
10 Golden Square, London W1R 3AF
Orchard Books Australia
14 Mars Road, Lane Cove NSW 2066
1 85213 013 X
Printed in Italy

a is for astronauts, apples and alligators

b is for balloons, bananas, bread, boots and balls

c is for clowns, cats, cups and cushions

d is for ducks, dinosaurs, dolls, donkeys and dolphins

e is for elephants and eggs

f is for flags, fish, flamingoes, feathers and fireworks

g is for giraffes, glasses and grass

h is for helicopters, houses, hats, hamburgers and horses

i is for ice-creams

j is for jack-in-the-boxes

k is for kangaroos and kites

l is for lighthouse, leaves, lions and lemons

m is for monkeys

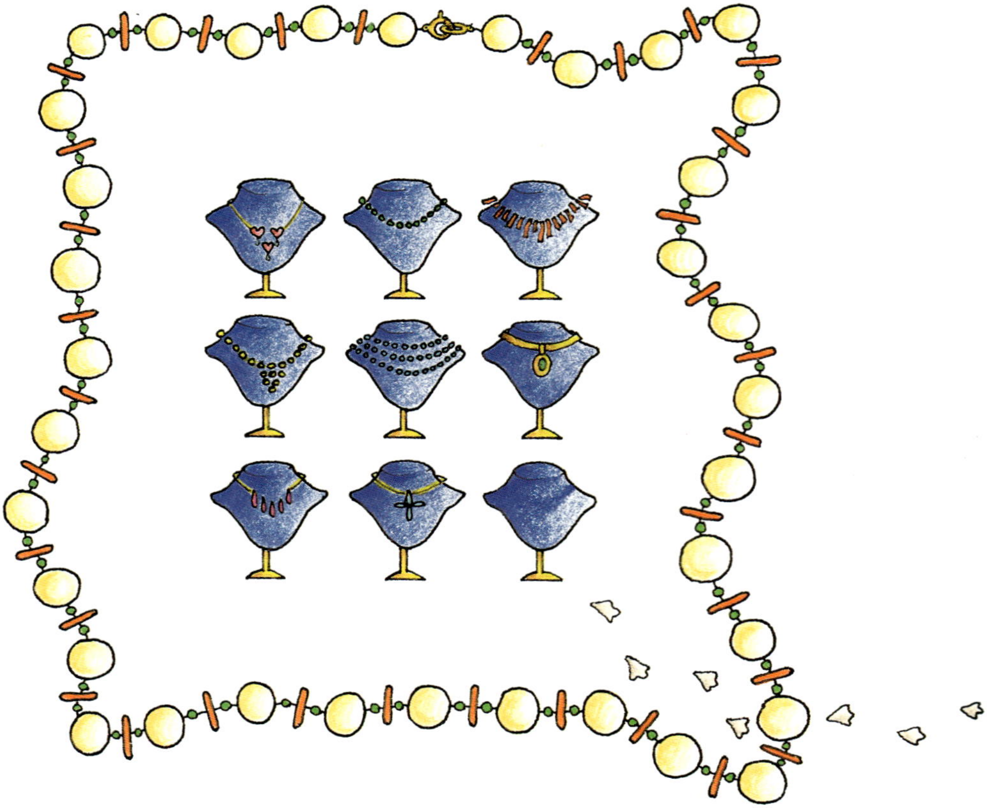

n is for necklaces and newspaper

o is for owls, oranges, octopus and ostriches

p is for puppets, parrots, pears and pandas

q is for queen and quilt

r is for rainbow, roses, rings, rope, rabbits and rocking-horses

s is for sun, starfish, sandwiches, snake, socks and sausages

t is for tortoises, twins, tomatoes, teddybears and toadstools

u is for umbrellas and unicorn

v is for volcanoes, violets, violins and van

w is for witches and wizards

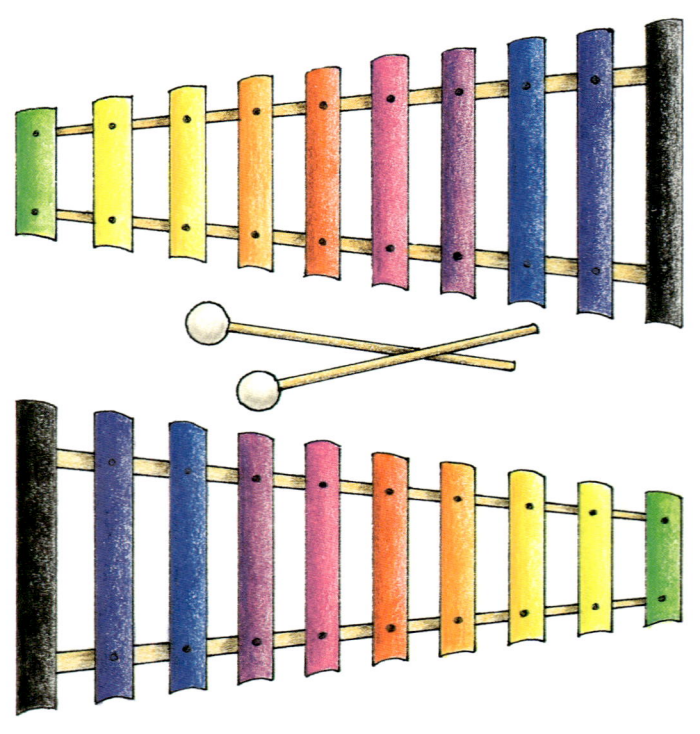

x is for xylophones

y is for yachts

z is for zoo